The 10 Sales Commandments

Take Immediate Control of your Life and Financial Destiny and Change your life forever with this Powerful Book

by

Oliver P. Maldonado

authorHOUSE

AuthorHouse™
1663 Liberty Drive
Bloomington, IN 47403
www.authorhouse.com
Phone: 833-262-8899

Published by AuthorHouse 10/08/2025

ISBN: 978-1-4208-0812-4 (sc)
ISBN: 978-1-4685-1049-2 (e)

Print information available on the last page.

I will not give up and I will persist until I accomplish and reach my goals.

No matter what dragons I will have to face and encounter, I am a dragon slayer and I will persist until I have slain each and every dragon that dares to test my will;

I will never quit because I don't know what that word means. I will not acknowledge such a word unless they are my goals who realize that it is inevitable and it will be my goals who quit making me chase them since they have realized they are being chased by the worlds most persistent human being that has ever lived.

From the 3rd Sales Commandment
In
The 10 Sales Commandments

I dedicate this book to the human spirit that is within all of us that will not give up regardless of what they may encounter along the path of the greatest adventure in the world "Life" in pursuit of Greatness!

The 10 Sales Commandments is from a Chapter in "The Greatest Sales Book in the World" by Oliver Maldonado.

Oliver Maldonado is nationally recognized as an Expert on Sales and is a National Sales Consultant and Sales Trainer who is currently on a National Campaign conducting Seminars that is guaranteed to increase his attendees sales by at least 30%.

He turned a simple recipe into $Millions!

Broke and alone and only having the strong desire to succeed and using the principals of The 10 Sales Commandments, Colonel Sanders went out and began door knocking and selling his recipe to restaurants and built an organization that in the year 2000 had an annual sales volume of $8.9 Billion Dollars.

When the Colonel first started out on his mission he didn't own a restaurant, he wasn't a young man he didn't have an education he only had a strong desire to succeed. How could someone that didn't even own a restaurant be able to create the empire that he had created? Well he was one of the greatest salespeople in the world, but his desire to succeed is what made him. When he first went out meeting with restaurants and their owners he got rejected. He got rejected a lot, in fact he got rejected over 1,000 times before he got his first yes! Now I know many people would have given up by the 9th or even 20th no! But that is what having a strong determination does, it gets you what you want!

When the Colonel first went out, he had this great recipe and he started visiting restaurants traveling around the country and he would promise the restaurants more profit than they had ever seen if they used his secret recipe. Most restaurants at the time were burger restaurants and he was not only persuading the restaurant owners to use his secret recipe but to change their entire restaurants menu, meaning this was a chicken recipe so the restaurant would have to switch from selling burgers to selling chicken.

The Colonel was right and all restaurants he serviced with his recipe did experience more success than they had experienced before.

He did this for many years and he had a lot of success. Without owning a single restaurant he had over 1,200 restaurant accounts that he provided his secret recipe for.

As you know, the Colonel also revolutionized the restaurant industry and created one of the most successful fast food franchises in the world. Kentucky Fried Chicken (KFC) has a unique product virtually unmatched today. There are many fast food chains, but not many chicken fast food chains.

The Colonel was one of the greatest salespeople in the world who used the words of the 10 Sales Commandments to take his sales ability to a level unseen before.

You will now have the secrets to sales success revealed in The 10 Sales Commandments that have been proven over time.

For those of you that are ready to achieve a higher level of success and are willing and able to follow The 10 Sales Commandments you will acquire great riches and it won't come easy. It will take great determination and will power to make yourself follow through with The 10 Sales Commandments until you have followed them so thoroughly that you will literally become brain washed into transforming your life and your actions into the life you have always dreamed of. The only way for you to become wealthy with riches and personal satisfaction is by reading and rereading this book as many times as it takes until you start becoming wealthy. Once you begin reaping the rewards of your great determination and will power, you will then continue reading The 10 Sales Commandments until you have reached all of your dreams and then you will share this powerful information with your friends and family to help them become wealthy and rich as you did. The 10 Sales Commandments is a way of life you should follow it to become wealthy and gain riches.

Authors Preface

The 10 Sales Commandments has the potential to become one of the most influential sales books of all time in the area of financial independence and wealth beyond your wildest dreams.

This book was inspired and part of The Greatest Sales Book in the World by Oliver Maldonado who also disclosed his secret sales formula. Oliver Maldonado has had a great deal of sales success and has taught his sales formula to many sales people around the country who have also experienced sales success using his secrets. There has been over $2.2 Billion in gross sales generated using the principles from The Greatest Sales Book in the World.

Oliver Maldonado has spent his entire adult life studying and mastering the art of sales and now shares his findings with thousands of people of all walks of life, rich and poor alike. His wishes are that all people who read and study his message will trade their hard work, thoughts, ideas and persistence in return for riches. Hundreds if not thousands of people around the country have applied the principals of this book in return for personal wealth accumulation and riches.

These principals are proven, timeless and practical and are now available to everyone who has a great desire to accumulate wealth & riches.

You will find in each chapter of this book the many mentions of the accumulation of wealth and riches. You will now have the secret formula to sales success. The idea behind this book is to share the discoveries of the author with the people who do not have the time and resources to investigate how great sales people earn income in the sales industry. For years the author has believed that sales should be a required course in school. There is an amazingly large amount of people around the country who work in the sales industry each and every year, and there is no formal education on the subject of sales. He has a plan to create the first accredited sales school in the country that would give people in pursuit of wealth & riches the knowledge and education necessary to be able to attain wealth through sales. This would be a sales training course that would take a few weeks instead of years of education. It is also strongly believed that the information contained in this book can indeed change the industry of sales as we know it.

Sales is the highest paid career in the world. This is a fact! However, most people do not regard sales people as professionals, yet most successful sales people are as determined and dedicated as any doctor or lawyer in the country. Great salespeople practice their skills and are constantly studying their art. They go to endless amounts of seminars, they read many motivational books. They continue studying and learning their products to the point that the great sales people are the foremost experts of their products, yet the average person does not respect a great salesperson as they do their accountants and attorneys when they are in many cases at a level above that of an attorney or accountant.

Great salespeople unlike accountants, attorneys or doctors keep track of their sales ability. They track their results, and numbers don't lie. Great salespeople are constantly bettering themselves unlike most accountants, attorneys or doctors. I once asked an attorney what his success ratio was? How many cases did he win? He had no idea! I also asked several other attorneys the same question and they could not answer me either. I made several mistakes with attorneys before finding one that I trusted. So the next time you meet an attorney, accountant or doctor, know there is no real way to know if this is a good, great or bad professional. It is deceiving because most of them still earn good incomes and most regardless of their ability still charge $200-$300 dollars per hour.

The Ten Sales Commandments

If you had only one shot, only one opportunity to seize everything you've ever wanted, would you take it? Or would you let it pass you by?

If you had the secret formula to Sales Success would you use it?
What if you had the answers to all of your questions on success and happiness? Would you follow through?

What if I told you, you could have it all! You can have everything you ever wanted. All the information to success and happiness in the world is contained in this little yet powerful book just waiting for you! This is very true. If you read and apply the information contained in this book, you will have more success and riches than you ever dreamed possible! There is a catch though! If you want to reach all of the sales success you have been dreaming of you must follow the next 5 steps to success.

> 1st you will have to take a moment before reading this book and write down your 6 Month sales goal. If you don't have one, take a moment to think of one.
> 2nd you will have to take a moment again before reading this book and write down your 1 and 3 Year sales goal.
> 3rd you will have to read this book to its entirety.
> 4th you will have to apply everything you read in this book on a daily, weekly, monthly and yearly basis.

5th you will re-read this book over & over & over again until you have reached your 6 Month and 1-3 year sales goals.

You will be able to write your 6 month and 1-3 year sales goals right in this book. Please find the blank sections for you to write down and keep with you so you can have them available for review.

If you are committed to accumulating great wealth and riches and you are going to commit all of yourself to this pursuit then prepare yourself for a Great Journey!

Sylvester Stallone knew the power of these powerful words before they were written when he went door to door knocking on every single movie production company he could find. When he was pushing his movie script of Rocky, he pushed it for 7 long hard years. He went to some movie producers 2-3 and 4 times getting rejected, over and over again but he wouldn't stop. He knew he had something that would change his life forever if he could only get a movie producer to produce his script. This was also during a time when he had no money.

After many years of peddling the Rocky script finally someone wanted to buy it from him and offered him a considerable amount of money. They offered him $50,000 dollars for the script. He said he would only sell the script if he could be the main actor in the movie. They said no way, you have a horrible voice and you're not that great looking plus no one knows you. The movie would certainly fail if you were in it. You don't even have any acting experience. He turned them down. He was so convinced that he would become a star that although they offered him $50,000 dollars during a time when he was broke and had no money he was determined to become a movie star and was convinced he would be if only someone would buy his script and let him be the main actor.

The movie producers that had offered him $50,000 came back to him and said, we really love the script and would like to buy it so name your price. Sylvester Stallone said I told you I want to be the main actor in the film. They said no way, we told you the reasons why before, but we're ready to offer you $250,000 for your script and Sylvester Stallone turned them down again. Wow, is this guy nuts? Keep in mind that he is broke and has no money. He was so broke that he could not afford dog food for the dog he loved so he went to the corner of where he lived and sold the dog he loved for $25. He tried to sell if for $100 but only got $25 for the dog. He really didn't have to sell his dog, he could have accepted the $250,000 and start a new life, but he was so determined and convinced that if he was the main actor he would be a movie star and earn $millions. This was also in the 1970's and although $250,000 dollars is a lot of money now, back then it was a fortune, but once again he was convinced and determined to become a movie star and become wealthier than he had ever imagined no matter what the cost.

Now months later the same movie producers came back and now offered him $750,000 dollars for the script and he still turned them down. The movie producers wanted the script so bad and realized he was not going to sell, they said okay. If you want to be the main actor in the movie then you are going to have to take the risk with us. We'll pay you what a regular new actor would earn $750 dollars a week and we'll give you some of the back end money on the gross of the movie. So this way if the movie fails because of you then you also lose money but if it makes money then you'll earn money. He finally accepted their offer and he was right. The movie turned out to be a huge hit with a budget of only $1 Million and grossing over $100 Million which helped make Sylvester Stallone a movie star. It has been a while since I've read that information so please don't quote me in those numbers, but they are close.

Sylvester Stallone knew and followed the powerful steps in this book until he finally reached more success than he ever thought possible. In one of his interviews, he states that "Sometimes he can't believe everything he has and all he has accomplished and that sometimes he just runs around his home screaming with excitement about how happy he is". Sylvester Stallone obviously knows the importance of the powerful secrets contained in this book. Sylvester Stallone is someone who has lived it from his own experience and can teach many of the secrets of success.

Some of the other great successes of our time are people such as Arnold Schwarzenegger. Arnold is someone who has accomplished so much in his lifetime. He has been the best at everything he has set his mind to. Arnold is obviously someone who has also mastered The 10 Sales Commandments. Arnold had a lot more challenges to overcome than most people that will be reading this book. He had language barriers to overcome. He came to a new country having no friends or family and no money. He then became the best bodybuilder of his time and some consider him the best bodybuilder of all time not to mention he also became a movie star, Entrepreneur, business owner and the Governor of California.

What most people don't realize is that he was not just the most successful bodybuilder of his time and in my opinion all time but also a very smart business person well before he became a movie star. He had written one of the most successful bodybuilding encyclopedias ever written! He self marketed this book himself which he had advertised in magazines like shirts and posters of his great physique. He also had many other products he also marketed in magazines. He self promoted himself into a fortune and this was well before he was in any movies.

But then he takes it a step further and becomes one of the best actors of all time. His movies have grossed over $3.4 Billion. He still continues to be one of the best businessmen in the country if not the world regardless of his movies. Most people would be happy being a movie star but he pushes himself to be the best he could be at all times which is why he is worth about $600 Million dollars. There are many movie stars around, but hardly any of them are as wealthy or worth $600 Million which is because they are happy and content just being wealthy. Many of them unfortunately end up broke in the end because they did not reinvent themselves and when they become unpopular and the movies are gone they don't have a way to earn the large amounts of money they once earned.

Arnold owns a lot of very expensive real estate and I am not referring to his homes, I'm referring to his commercial buildings that he owns around the country. Arnold obviously knows the art of negotiation negotiating several of the best paychecks in Hollywood. He also negotiated a 747 Jetliner worth over $100 million dollars instead of a paycheck for one of his movies. Arnold is another amazing individual who knows all of the secrets to success contained in this book.

I've mentioned these two very high profile individuals because I'm sure most of you will recognize the names but might be surprised about some of their accomplishments and believe me I didn't scratch the surface on most of their accomplishments.

That being said, allow me to mention a couple of other great men that also followed The 10 Sales Commandments well before the book was published but which was also a major inspiration by these men and their actions and accomplishments that helped create this book.

Ray Crok is one of those men. Although many might not know who Ray Crok is by his name alone, most if not everyone has bought his products at one point or another. Ray Crok was an amazing salesperson who revolutionized the fast food industry. Before Ray Crok there really was no fast food restaurants. His story is an amazing one. Ray Crok was not originally in the restaurant business, he was originally a salesperson selling multi-mixers which was a blender that had 3 to 5 sections to make more milkshakes. That's how he met the McDonalds brothers who he had heard had a restaurant that was selling more burgers than any other restaurant had ever sold before. Ray Crok originally just wanted to sell more multi-mixers and that is why he helped the McDonald brothers open up more restaurants and eventually he bought them out and the rest as you know is history!

Ray Crok was already a successful salesperson before he met the McDonalds brothers and before he revolutionized the restaurant and fast food industry.

Ray Crok is another person who was an amazing salesperson and a genius on the principals contained in the 10 Sales Commandments! Ray Crok has never read this information, but believe me when I tell you he knows these principals all too well which is how he was able to realize his wildest dreams, beyond anything he ever dreamed of.

If you can follow the 5 easy steps you will be guaranteed more success in sales than you have ever imagined. This is not a joke. You must believe in everything you are about to read and you must know that you can and will reach your 6 Month and 1-3 year sales goals. With the success of reaching your 6 Month goals you will start building the confidence needed to reach your 1-3 year sales goals. If you are unable to reach your 6 Month sales goal within the 1st 6 Months, then you must realize that you did not follow the 5 steps above. The only way you will not reach your 6 Month sales goals is by not following the 5 steps to sales success.

Do not be discouraged if you do not reach your 6 month sales goals. If you did not reach your 6 month sales goals, you can start all over. But you will have to start with your 6 month sales goals. If you would like you can adjust your 6 month sales goals and follow the 5 steps to sales success until you have reached your 6 month sales goals. You cannot attempt to try and reach your 1-3 year sales goals until you have first reached your 6 month sales goals. This is the only way to create the kind of success you have only dreamed of. This will be the foundation needed to reach all of your future sales goals.

This is a very important step for you to become a successful salesperson and reach all of the sales successes you have only dreamed of until this point. So remember this is not a compromise. You must and will reach your 6 month sales goals and then your 1-3 year sales goals. Do not move on to your 1-3 year sales goals no matter how close you have come to reaching the 6 month sales goals first. Do not re-adjust your 6 month sales goals until after attempting to reach it. If you must adjust your 6 month sales goals you can do so, but you must start from scratch once you've adjusted it.

The 10 Sales Commandments will be your guide to riches beyond your wildest dreams. You will keep this book with you everywhere you go. Keep it in your briefcase, your car, your home. Keep it with you at all times and when you have a little bit of extra time you will pull it out and read it to yourself. You will first start reading your 6 month sales goals and then your 1-3 year sales goals. You will read and follow the 5 steps to sales success and you will know that you will continue reading and following the 5 steps until you have reached your 6 month sales goals.

There are 2 blank sections following this section where you will write down your 6 month and 1-3 year sales goals. This will help hold you accountable. But you must remember to follow the 5 steps to sales success. Don't wait another minute make the first step to reaching riches beyond your wildest dreams. Commit to following the 5 steps to sales success now. Do not wait! Do not put this off another minute! Do not lie to yourself and tell yourself that you will commit to it when the time is right! In reality the time will never be as right as it is right now. So be grateful that you have this amazing opportunity before you and make this your defining moment.

For years we have all heard if the right opportunity came along we would jump on it and not let it pass us by. You have already passed the point of return. You have now read too much of The 10 Sales Commandments to stop now. Now that you have read this much, let it be known that this is your right opportunity and you will live a life of absolute regret if you let your right opportunity, this one pass you by without following through all the way to the end. You will have a lingering self doubt in your mind that will not go away. You will always know that there was something you did not complete or accomplish that you know you could have, but that you let the biggest opportunity of your life pass you by. You will be haunted by the thoughts and dreams of what could have happened, no, what should have been had you only followed through.

You can always come back to this book and complete it at a later date, but why not complete it now. Meet the challenge head on!

This is not a huge request, this is a fairly small book that will change your life forever, but only if you commit to following the 5 steps to sales success right now and apply The 10 Sales Commandments.

Resistance is futile!

I have been contacted by many sales people around the world that have told me they had been haunted by not following through with the 5 steps of sales success from the 10 sales commandments and what they should do in order to be able to get rid of the torture that haunts them regarding their lack of follow through. I will tell you as I have told them, the only way you will be able to move on with a sense of accomplishment and piece of mind is by following through with the 5 steps to sales success. This is the only way for you to have any piece of mind. There are no hidden secrets than simply following through and completing the 5 steps to sales success.

Do not fall into the "should've" category. I should've followed through, I should've read the whole book, I should've reached my 6 month sales goals, I should've followed the 5 steps to sales success. Anthony Robbins says it best in his "Awaken the Giant Within" when he said that's what he says is like "Should've all over yourself". So don't should've all over yourself. Nike says it best when they say "Just do it"!

Even if you are currently experiencing sales success at the moment, you should know that the success you will attain after reading this book will be the ones you have only dreamt of. All sales people need this book even the ones experiencing great sales success at the moment.

Salespeople have their ups and downs, good and bad days, months and even years and the only way to stay sharp and consistent is by continuing to better yourself at all times. Doctors, Lawyers, CPA's and Financial Planners all have continuing education that they must complete in order for them to maintain their success.

I believe that great salespeople are as committed or even more committed to their profession than a Doctor or Lawyer. The average salesperson may not be, but they are also the ones just trying out sales and have not committed themselves to it as a career and only represent about 15-20 percent of all sales done in the world. I also believe that Doctors and Lawyers are Salespeople also and the great professionals will also read this book and they will achieve even a greater level of success than other Doctors or Lawyers after they have read this book.

The 1ˢᵗ Sales Commandment

Today I've decided to start a new life.

The only thing I can control in this world is me and today I've decided to start a new life and leave my old life behind. In my old life I suffered, struggled and failed for too long. If I continued down the path of my old life, I would have been doomed to live a life of mediocrity, struggle, and misery so today I decide to start a new life.

Today I decide to start a new life.

Today I will start a new life where everything is possible. Today I've realized that the career I have chosen is paved with gold and riches beyond my wildest dreams and there is nothing but opportunity awaiting me and I will succeed. Today I have realized that I have failed in the past and there will be many more people who will fail in front of me like doomed men giving up creating large piles of doomed souls in front of me which will not have any affect on me, and I will not fail like the others for I have already failed for too long and today I decide to start a new life.

I've put in my dues and already given years of struggle and failure and I will no longer accept that as my reality. Failure will now be foreign to me and I will no longer tolerate or accept struggle as payment for success. Now I will reject failure and I am prepared to accept success as my payment for my past struggles. I will use what I've learned over the years and what I will learn from this book and I demand everything that is due to me in full and with interest. My time is now and I will only accept success, wealth, riches and happiness beyond my wildest dreams as payment in full.

Today I decided to start a new life and my determination to succeed is strong enough to get me there. I will not fail and I will use everything in my power to reach a level of wealth, success, riches and happiness larger than I had even imagined it in my dreams.

Today I decided to start a new life and I know no matter what happens, good or bad what an adventure it will be.

Today I decided to start a new life!

The 2ⁿᵈ Sales Commandment

I will start each day by being positive and having a great attitude.

I have begun a new life and in this new life, I will be positive with a great attitude. In order for me to succeed and acquire the riches and happiness that is due me in my new life, I must always be amazingly positive and exude a great attitude.

I will receive and I expect resistance from others regarding my new positive and great attitude, but I know that neither my co-workers nor prospects nor close relatives will be able to resist my contagious positive and great attitude.

I am exited to have come to this defining moment and I have accepted the challenge to make all of my wildest dreams a reality by starting each day by being positive and having a great attitude.

I will start each day by being positive and having a great attitude since I am on the doorsteps of greatness. My time is now and there is absolutely no reason why not to feel and be positive with a great attitude since I am well on my way to reaching all of my dreams. Why would someone destined for greatness be anything less than positive with a great attitude? Someone destined for greatness would never be anything less than positive with a great attitude and since I am also destined for greatness and amazing success I will start each day by doing the same and being positive with a great attitude.

Today is going to be a great day!

I will face today and everyday knowing that it will be a great day since I am the master of each day and how the day plays out I will make today and every day that follows a great day.

I will make today and everyday forward a great day. I and only I alone can control my emotions and feelings and I am also the master of my days and I will make it a great day for today is the only day I can make great at this very moment therefore the only day I can and will make great is today.

I will start each day by being positive and having a great attitude and I will infect anyone and everyone who near me with my positive thinking and great attitude!

The 3ʳᵈ Sales Commandment

I will not give up and I will persist until I accomplish and reach my goals.

Although I will encounter many obstacles in my path to greatness and the world will try to stop me. I will not allow them to deter me. I will not give up. I know that these obstacles I will face will be more than many men or women can handle yet they will not deter me for even a millionth of a second. No matter what dragons I will have to face and encounter, I am a dragon slayer and I will persist until I have slain each and every dragon that dares to test my will and I will persist until I accomplish and reach my goals. I will never quit because I don't know what that word means. I will not acknowledge such a word unless they are my goals who realize that it is inevitable and it will be my goals who quit making me chase them since they have realized they are being chased by the worlds most persistent human being that has ever lived.

I will persist until I accomplish and reach my goals.

I will not quit and when I need motivation I will refer to this motivating poem by an unknown poet. This poem is refreshing and although I do not know who wrote the poem I know it must have been written by someone who has also persisted and has reached their goals. I know the person who wrote this very powerful poem has seen their own share of dragons and was successful in slaying all dragons who appeared before them and like them I will do the same and in a time of weakness, I will look to this poem and find the needed strength that will help me accomplish and reach my goals.

Don't Quit

When things go wrong as they
sometimes will,
When the road you're trudging seems
all up hill, When the funds are low and
the debts are high, And you want to
smile, but you have to sigh, When care is
pressing you down a bit,
Rest if you must, but don't you quit!
Success is failure turned inside out,
The silver tint on the clouds of doubt,
And you never can tell how close you
are, It may be near when it seems afar;
So stick to the fight when you're hardest
hit. I's when things seem wors that you
musn't qui!t!!

The 4th Sales Commandment

I must create lasting change in my life.

I have realized that what I have been doing has not worked for me. If I continue doing the things that have not worked, I will fail. I will not succeed. I will be considered a failure, a looser. If I do not change I will suffer and feel immediate, unbearable and devastating amounts of pain, so I must change.

I must create lasting change in my life.

I have already been told by my friends, family and the world that I cannot change. That I cannot achieve. I am well aware that they have become numb by their own past failures. I know they have been brain washed by society and they have also been conditioned to what they cannot do. I will not follow in their footsteps and allow them to attempt to brainwash me. I will not become numb to their voices and words of failure. I will not allow them to speak such nonsense around me and tell me what they think I cannot do. When anyone including my family, friends, co-workers and acquaintances try to convince me on the things I cannot do, I will correct them and tell them I can, will and must change things in my life to achieve all of my goals in life.

I must create lasting change in my life.

I will feed from my successes. Small successes in the beginning will be just enough nourishment to keep me from starving, but the effects have triggered a reaction I will not be able to control. The changes I will have made in my life have triggered these senses within me that are uncontrollable. I will have become addicted to the sensation of my successes that are now stacking atop each other. Each success makes me stronger than the last. With each success, my hunger for more success grows and grows. I will feed from my successes which I will need in order to survive. The lasting changes I have made in my life will bring me more material things and finances which have made my family, friends and acquaintances believe in me. Now they are also making changes in their lives to try and follow my footsteps. I must create lasting change in my life so I can not only help myself but also the people I care about the most which will also bring me the most amount of happiness and pleasure that will help feed my appetite.

I must create lasting change in my life.

The 5ᵗʰ Sales Commandment

I will live today to the Fullest!

On this day I choose to live it to the fullest I can possibly live it. Since I will live this day to the fullest, I will have no time to waste on worrying about my past failures. I have learned from my failures and I appreciate the lessons I have learned from them. My past failures have made me a stronger, better wiser salesperson so I will live today to the fullest and have the assurance that my past failures were necessary to get me to this day which is a step closer to reaching all my goals and dreams. For that I am grateful and I will live today to the fullest.

I will not worry about tomorrow. I cannot live today to the fullest and achieve everything I must and reach my goals today if I have the worry about tomorrow clouding my judgment today. Therefore I will not worry about tomorrow today. In order for me to reach tomorrow I must finish out today and today I will live to the fullest. Since I will live today to the fullest and achieve my goals today, I know that my actions today will better tomorrow. With the confidence and knowledge of knowing my actions today will better tomorrow, I will not worry about tomorrow.

I will live today to the fullest.

The only thing I can control in this world is myself and what I do today. I will live today to the fullest and reach my goals which will make all of my dreams come true.

I will live today to the fullest.

The 6ᵗʰ Sales Commandment

I will control my emotions everyday.

I cannot control many things in life. Things are constantly changing in my world. People come and go, acquaintances fade, the seasons change, children grow up, economies change, and the world around me will continue to change forever. I cannot control many things in the world around me except myself. The only thing I can control in this world is me and how I feel and I will control my emotions everyday.

Emotions are merely definitions each individual person gives to how they are feeling. Emotions are not planted in me, other than the definition I give it myself. When a difficult or bad situation arises in my life, I can feel to get frustrated or mad or I can merely look at it as a challenge and control my emotions to find a more productive way to meet the challenge before me. Either way I look at it, the situation itself will remain the self regardless of which emotion I choose to feel. I am the master of my emotions and which emotion I choose to feel is up to me and only me and I will control my emotions everyday. There are emotions that can empower me and emotions that can dis-empower me and I will control my emotions everyday and choose the emotions that will empower me to overcome anything I will encounter each day. I choose to be wise and select the emotion that will empower me which will help me in each situation I encounter. Sometimes I may select to be happy while other times I may need to feel determined to accomplish a task. No matter what emotions I feel whether it be happy, determined, persistent, energetic or even peeved sometimes

I will control my emotions everyday and select the emotion that will empower me. In situations when a negative emotion has caught me by surprise I will know immediately that is not the most optimum emotion and I since I am the only one who can control my emotions I will select a better empowering emotion.

I am the master of my emotions and I will control my emotions everyday!

The 7th Sales Commandment

I will live my life as a happy energetic person.

Happy energetic people have the most friends and fun than everyone else. In actuality happy energetic people have the most of everything. They have more friends because most people want to be around someone that is happy and energetic. Even people they do not know are constantly attracted to them always approaching them to speak with them whether in an elevator, convention or park, happy energetic people are contagious and always attract others to them, so they are constantly making new friends. I will live my life as a happy energetic person. They have the greatest relationships business and personal. Happy energetic people have the most business and clientele because they attract other people who want to be around them and work with them, so like them I will live life as a happy energetic person. Since I will live my life as a happy energetic person I will have the most friends and that will make me a happier person. By being happy and energetic I will also start making friends with new business associates and I will also start acquiring more and more clients and my clients will then refer me to more prospects since they will want their friends and family to be around someone as happy and energetic like me.

I will live my life as a happy energetic person.

There is much more to living my life as a happy energetic person than just making new friends, having more relationships and clients. I will also be able to affect and influence in a positive way all of the people I care about the most. My loved ones will benefit from my new happy energetic personality and I will be able to brighten their lives which in turn will brighten my life even more. My new contagious happy energetic personality will soon rub off on them and they too will live happier more energetic lives and that will affect their other loved ones and their relationships.

I will live my life as a happy energetic person.

Although there will be challenging times ahead, I will live my life as a happy energetic person and which will help overcome the challenges I am sure to face in the future.

Living as a happy energetic person will be a way of life. Soon I will not know the difference and being happy and energetic will be as normal to me as breathing is to me.

I will live my life as a happy and energetic person.

The 8th Sales Commandment

I will multiply myself and increase my value.

At one point or another everyone has wished they could duplicate or clone themselves. We've wished that so that we can work and sleep at the same time. So we could earn more money or sell to more people in the same time period. I've wished that I could multiply myself so I could duplicate my results dramatically and increase my value. I've never wished to multiply myself for the good things like, have an extra me around on vacation. Or have two of me sleeping in my bed at the same time. Every time I've ever wanted to multiply myself has always been to increase production, more sales so I could increase my value and now I will be able to multiply myself and increase my value. The greatest sales people in the world and successful people in general have learned the secret of multiplicity that has increased their values. They've learned how to multiply themselves which multiplies their results which in turn gives them more production, sales, money and even more time having fun with family and friends so I will multiply myself and increase my value.

I will multiply myself and increase my value.

Today I will work harder and smarter, not one or the other but both are necessary to multiply myself and increase my value. I will come up with and implement new ideas that will increase my production. I will master my products, tools and presentations so that my conversion ratios increase dramatically.

I will multiply myself and increase my value.

By mastering my products, tools and presentations I will be able to multiply myself. I will speak of my products and services so well that everyone I have spoken with will be able to duplicate what I have said to them with their family and friends. They will remember my powerful presentation and come back to meet with me again for added products and services and they will bring their family and friends. My associates will know I am the master of our products, tools and services and will also refer others to me knowing I am a master at what we do and wanting to provide the best for everyone whom they send my way which they will be rewarded with the knowledge of knowing they were still able to help everyone they have sent to me. I will reap the rewards of multiplicity that will also come when I've increased my value, and my income will begin multiplying itself. The quarters will turn to dollars and the dollars will turn to five dollars and the five to ten, and ten to one hundred and I will reap the rewards of my increased value.

I will multiply myself and increase my value.

The 9th Sales Commandment

I am in control of my destiny and I will take action now.

None of my dreams and goals will ever amount to anything unless I take action now. I will not reach any of my dreams unless I act upon my dreams and goals. The only action that is important is the one I take now. My past actions will not help me in this moment so I must act now. My future actions will not help me at this very moment either and since I am in control of my destiny I will take action now.

I am in control of my destiny and I will take action now.

Nothing in this world that has ever been achieved or accomplished has come from procrastination. Procrastination is the force of all evil therefore I will not procrastinate and I will take action now. Everything in this world has come from someone taking action. The chair you sit in, someone took action and designed and built it. The streets you drive on, your home, your auto, everything in this world came from someone taking action. Even this book I am reading came from my action.

I am in control of my destiny and I will take action now.

All of my past accomplishments and achievements came from my actions, so I will take action now to accomplish and achieve even greater levels of success that to this point I have only dreamed of. The only reason I have not been able to achieve more in the past has been from my inability to take action then. If I would have taken action and studied my products and services more, I would have been more successful and earned more which is why I will take action now. If I would have taken action on my presentations I would have increased my conversion ratios therefore closing more deals and earning more income for myself and the company. If I would have taken action on my goals, dreams and ideas I would have achieved more than I have, therefore I will procrastinate no longer and I will take action now.

I understand that my procrastination has hindered me which has resulted in added struggle and less wealth which the realization now is feeding my hunger to act now and create more success and wealth for myself and the company and I will procrastinate no longer.

I am in control of my destiny and I will take action now.

The 10th Sales Commandment

I will be flexible and continually change my approach until I reach my destination.

A plane is of course over 90% of the time, yet it reaches its final destination each and every time. The plane continually changes its direction over and over and over again until it has reached its destination. Just as an airplane continually changes its approach to reach its destination so will I be flexible and change my approach until I reach my destination. Someone once said the definition of insanity is doing the same thing over and over again and expecting a different result. If something is not working for me, I must change my approach and I should not continue to do the same thing over and over again and expect a different result so I will be flexible and continually change my approach until I've reached my destination.

I will be flexible and continually change my approach until I reach my destination.

Just because I have failed in the past does not mean I will fail in the future, and my past failures cannot affect me or hold me back from reaching my goals and attaining riches, wealth and happiness. Just because I have failed in the past does not mean I will not be able to reach my dreams and goals although many would have me believe that.

Many people including my family and friends will constantly remind me of my past failures and try to convince me that I cannot succeed because of the past. I will remind myself and all of them that my past does not equal my future. If my determination to succeed is strong enough failure will never overtake me! I will continue to change my approach just like the greatest men in the world did. Just like Thomas Edison who was asked on his 9,999th attempt at inventing the light bulb if he thought he would fail again on the 10,000th attempt. Edison's reply was he hadn't failed 9,999 times, but discovered 9,999 ways not to invent the light bulb. Like Thomas Edison I will continue attempting new ways to achieve my goals and I will continue to change my approach even if it takes me 10,000 different changes to reach all of my goals because when I reach my destination all of the changes it took will have been worth all of the effort it took!

I will have challenges and I will overcome them. I will hear my friends, family and acquaintances tell me what they think I cannot do, but I will be flexible and continually change my approach until I reach my destination. Some of what I will do and have done may not have worked in getting me to my destination and that is exactly why I will be flexible and continually change my approach until I reach my destination.

I will be flexible and continually change my approach until I reach my destination.

I have read the 10 Sales Commandments and will continue to read each and everyday until I achieve everything I have set out to achieve. Sales can be the highest paid hard work or the lowest paid easy work. This is the profession I have chosen to be in and I can and will achieve all of my goals. I will reach all of my dreams.

I will follow the 10 sales commandments until I have reaped the rewards from the fruits of my labor that await me.

I choose to be a success and choose not to be a failure. The only way I fail is if I give up and that is something I will not do.

I do this not to prove anything to anyone else but myself. I choose to be a huge success and have more than I imagined possible not because of others but for myself. I do this to prove it to myself that first I can accomplish my mission and second for all of the rewards I will receive when I have accomplished what I have set out to accomplish.

I will do what ever it takes to succeed. The only failure there is, is giving up and I know I will not give up so I will succeed.

I have completed reading this powerful book filled of the secrets to sales success and I will continue to read this book on a daily, weekly and monthly basis until I have evolved into the Salesperson I want to be.

I know if I follow the 10 sales commandments I will reap the rewards and have riches beyond my wildest dreams.

I will continue to follow the 10 Sales Commandments until I have made all of my dreams a reality.

Here are My 6 Month Goals I Must Reach!

Date:_____
Within 6 Months I Must, _____

_____

_____

_____

_____

_____

_____

_____

_____

Within 6 Months I Must Have, _____

_____

_____

_____

_____

_____

_____

_____

Within 6 Months I Must Earn, _____

_____

_____

_____

_____

_____

_____

_____

_____

Within 6 Months I Must Achieve, _____

_____

_____

_____

_____

_____

_____

_____

Notes: _____

_____

_____

_____

_____

_____

_____

_____

_____

_____

_____

_____

_____

Here are My 1 Year Goals I Must Reach!

Date:_____
Within 1 Year I Must, _____

_____
_____
_____
_____
_____
_____
_____
_____
_____

Within 1 Year I Must Have, _____

_____
_____
_____
_____
_____
_____
_____
_____

Within 1 Year I Must Earn,_____

_____
_____
_____
_____
_____

_____

_____

_____

Within 1 Year I Must Achieve,_____

_____

_____

_____

_____

_____

_____

_____

Notes: _____

_____

_____

_____

_____

_____

_____

_____

_____

_____

_____

_____

Here are My 3 Year Goals I Must Reach!

Date:_____

Within 3 Years I Must, _____

_____

_____

_____

_____

_____

_____

_____

_____

Within 3 Years I Must Have, _____

_____

_____

_____

_____

_____

_____

_____

_____

Within 3 Years I Must Earn, _____

_____

_____

_____

_____

_____

_____

_____

_____

Within 3 Years I Must Achieve, _____

_____

_____

_____

_____

_____

_____

_____

Notes: _____

_____

_____

_____

_____

_____

_____

_____

_____

_____

_____

_____

_____

_____

_____

Success should be tracked in order to see how you succeeded and be able to Duplicate your success!

In the next section that follows you will find some blank sheets for you to fill out tracking how you were able to reach your 6 month and 1-3 year goals. If you did not reach all of your goals just track the goals you did reach and explain what you did in order to reach your goals.

Failure like Success should be tracked in order to learn what you did wrong and learn how not to repeat your mistakes!

If at first you don't succeed? Try and try again!

Some of you may have been aggressive with your goals. Don't worry and don't be discouraged if you didn't reach your goals. I too have always set my goals at levels that were higher than what I originally gave enough time for and sometimes didn't reach them right away. I am always impressed with someone who is willing to challenge themselves to reach something that has been out of their reach. Anyone can achieve goals they already know they can do.

If you don't set high goals for yourself you'll never really know what you can do. So everyone should attempt to reach something that may be a little out of their reach and by doing this you will reach higher levels of success even when you don't reach your goal fully!

None the less, I have included some extra blank 6 month and 1-3 year goal sheets for you to fill out.

As you have already read in this book, Colonel Sanders got rejected over 1,000 times before getting his first yes.

Thomas Edison attempted to invent the light bulb over 10,000 times before finally inventing the light bulb and changing his world and the world we know.

It will take many temporary defeats in order to reach any worth while goal! So how many times did you try to reach the goals you have set for yourself?

How many temporary defeats did you go through?

Did you attempt only once? If you only attempted once, then you really didn't even try. You must be persistent until you've reached your goals! You must attempt 50 times, or even 200 times, or maybe you'll have to try 600 times, and in some cases it may even take 1,000's of tries to reach greatness. But it is well worth it! Don't give up! Get back to your goals and start all over! Keep trying until you've reached your goals!

Here is a chart you can follow for you to see exactly how many times you really tried to reach your goals. Anything other than at least 20 separate attempts is really not trying that hard at all.

If you reached your goals within 10 attempts, then you should also re-write your goals, they were set too low for your ability although some goals may be reached within a short amount of attempts, some. If you've reached most of your goals within 10 attempts, then congratulations! But you should really consider re-writing your goals to see what you're really capable of achieving. Challenge yourself to be greater!

For each attempt circle a single 1 on the sheet that follows. After you've reached your goals then add up all of the circled 1's and see how many attempts it took you to reach your goals. If you haven't reached your goals by the end then add up all of the circled 1's and start over on the following section. If by the 2nd section you haven't reached your goals with all of the attempts, then it's time to re-write your goals. They may be too aggressive.

This is an exercise that is extremely affective to hold yourself accountable and for you to see and realize how much actual effort it will take for you to reach your goals. Be honest with yourself! Don't try to trick yourself, the purpose of reading this book and following these exercises is to reach wealth and riches beyond your wildest dreams and you'll never be able to reach them if you lie or mislead yourself!

So follow the instructions and get out there and start reaching your goals!

My Attempts Chart

1st Set of Attempts of 100 Total (s)

1 1 1 1 1 1 1 1 1 1 1 1 1 1 1 1 1 1 1 1_____
1 1 1 1 1 1 1 1 1 1 1 1 1 1 1 1 1 1 1 1_____
1 1 1 1 1 1 1 1 1 1 1 1 1 1 1 1 1 1 1 1_____
1 1 1 1 1 1 1 1 1 1 1 1 1 1 1 1 1 1 1 1_____
1 1 1 1 1 1 1 1 1 1 1 1 1 1 1 1 1 1 1 1_____

Total Attempts _____

_____

2nd 1st Set of Attempts of 100 Total (s)

1 1 1 1 1 1 1 1 1 1 1 1 1 1 1 1 1 1 1 1_____
1 1 1 1 1 1 1 1 1 1 1 1 1 1 1 1 1 1 1 1_____
1 1 1 1 1 1 1 1 1 1 1 1 1 1 1 1 1 1 1 1_____
1 1 1 1 1 1 1 1 1 1 1 1 1 1 1 1 1 1 1 1_____
1 1 1 1 1 1 1 1 1 1 1 1 1 1 1 1 1 1 1 1_____

Total Attempts _____

_____

3rd 1st Set of Attempts of 100 Total (s)

1 1 1 1 1 1 1 1 1 1 1 1 1 1 1 1 1 1 1 1_____
1 1 1 1 1 1 1 1 1 1 1 1 1 1 1 1 1 1 1 1_____
1 1 1 1 1 1 1 1 1 1 1 1 1 1 1 1 1 1 1 1_____
1 1 1 1 1 1 1 1 1 1 1 1 1 1 1 1 1 1 1 1_____
1 1 1 1 1 1 1 1 1 1 1 1 1 1 1 1 1 1 1 1_____

Total Attempts _____

My Attempts Chart

2nd Set of Attempts of 100 Total (s)

1 1 1 1 1 1 1 1 1 1 1 1 1 1 1 1 1 1 1 1____
1 1 1 1 1 1 1 1 1 1 1 1 1 1 1 1 1 1 1 1____
1 1 1 1 1 1 1 1 1 1 1 1 1 1 1 1 1 1 1 1____
1 1 1 1 1 1 1 1 1 1 1 1 1 1 1 1 1 1 1 1____
1 1 1 1 1 1 1 1 1 1 1 1 1 1 1 1 1 1 1 1____

Total Attempts _____

2nd 2nd Set of Attempts of 100 Total (s)

1 1 1 1 1 1 1 1 1 1 1 1 1 1 1 1 1 1 1 1____
1 1 1 1 1 1 1 1 1 1 1 1 1 1 1 1 1 1 1 1____
1 1 1 1 1 1 1 1 1 1 1 1 1 1 1 1 1 1 1 1____
1 1 1 1 1 1 1 1 1 1 1 1 1 1 1 1 1 1 1 1____
1 1 1 1 1 1 1 1 1 1 1 1 1 1 1 1 1 1 1 1____

Total Attempts _____

3rd 2nd Set of Attempts of 100 Total (s)

1 1 1 1 1 1 1 1 1 1 1 1 1 1 1 1 1 1 1 1____
1 1 1 1 1 1 1 1 1 1 1 1 1 1 1 1 1 1 1 1____
1 1 1 1 1 1 1 1 1 1 1 1 1 1 1 1 1 1 1 1____
1 1 1 1 1 1 1 1 1 1 1 1 1 1 1 1 1 1 1 1____
1 1 1 1 1 1 1 1 1 1 1 1 1 1 1 1 1 1 1 1____

Total Attempts _____

Here is how I reached my 6 Month Goals!

Date:_____

Within 6 Months I was able to accomplish my goals by doing: Or

Within 6 Months I did not reach my goals because:

_____

_____

_____

_____

_____

_____

Within 6 Months I was able to acquire my goals by doing: Or

Within 6 Months I did not reach my goals because:

_____

_____

_____

_____

_____

_____

Within 6 Months I was able to Earn by doing: Or

Within 6 Months I did not reach my goals because:

_____

_____

_____

_____

_____

Within 6 Months I was able to Achieve by doing: Or
Within 6 Months I did not reach my goals because:

_____

_____

_____

_____

_____

Here is how I reached My 1 Year Goals!

Date:_____

Within 1 Year I was able to accomplish by doing: Or
Within 1 Year I did not reach my goals because:

_____
_____
_____
_____
_____
_____

Within 1 Year I was able to Acquire by doing: Or
Within 1 Year I did not reach my goals because:

_____
_____
_____
_____
_____
_____

Within 1 Year I was able to Earn by doing: Or
Within 1 Year I did not reach my goals because:

_____
_____
_____
_____
_____
_____

Within 1 Year I was able to Achieve by doing: Or
Within 1 Year I did not reach my goals because:

_____

_____

_____

_____

_____

Here is how I was Able to Reach My 3 Year Goals!

Date:_____

Within 3 Years I was able to Accomplish by doing: Or
Within 3 Years I did not reach my goals because:

_____
_____
_____
_____
_____
_____

Within 3 Years I was able to Acquire by doing: Or
Within 3 Years I did not reach my goals because:

_____
_____
_____
_____
_____
_____

Within 3 Years I was Able to Earn by doing: Or
Within 3 Years I did not reach my goals because:

_____
_____
_____
_____
_____
_____

Within 3 Years I was able to Achieve by doing: Or
Within 3 Years I did not reach my goals because:

_____

_____

_____

_____

_____

_____

Here are My New 6 Month Goals I Must Reach!

Date:_____

Within 6 Months I Must, _____

_____

_____

_____

_____

_____

_____

_____

_____

Within 6 Months I Must Have, _____

_____

_____

_____

_____

_____

_____

_____

Within 6 Months I Must Earn, _____

_____

_____

_____

_____

_____

_____

_____

_____

Within 6 Months I Must Achieve, _____

_____

_____

_____

_____

_____

_____

_____

Notes: _____

_____

_____

_____

_____

_____

_____

_____

_____

_____

_____

_____

_____

_____

_____

_____

Here are My New 1 Year Goals I Must Reach!

Date:_____

Within 1 Year I Must, _____

_____

_____

_____

_____

_____

_____

_____

_____

Within 1 Year I Must Have, _____

_____

_____

_____

_____

_____

_____

_____

_____

Within 1 Year I Must Earn, _____

_____

_____

_____

_____

_____

_____

_____

_____

Within 1 Year I Must Achieve, _____

_____

_____

_____

_____

_____

_____

_____

Notes: _____

_____

_____

_____

_____

_____

_____

_____

_____

_____

_____

_____

_____

_____

_____

Here are My New 3 Year Goals I Must Reach!

Date:_____
Within 3 Years I Must, _____

_____

_____

_____

_____

_____

_____

_____

_____

Within 3 Years I Must Have, _____

_____

_____

_____

_____

_____

_____

_____

_____

Within 3 Years I Must Earn, _____

_____

_____

_____

_____

_____

_____

_____

_____

Within 3 Years I Must Achieve, _____

_____

_____

_____

_____

_____

_____

_____

_____

Notes: _____

_____

_____

_____

_____

_____

_____

_____

_____

_____

_____

_____

_____

_____

Oliver Maldonado is one of the most sought after speakers and sales trainers in the country.

The 10 Sales Commandments is from a chapter in The Greatest Sales Book in the World which has generated over $2.2 Billion dollars in gross sales from the systems and material in the book.

If you would like to see one of Oliver Maldonado's Seminars visit OliverMaldonado.com to see when a seminar might be near you.

If you'd like information on Oliver Maldonado's consulting services or for his sales coaching you may also visit OliverMaldonado.com for additional information and to get in contact with the Author.

This book could be worth $1,000,000 One Million Dollars to you!

Learn what the Wealthiest people in the World know about creating Wealth and how you can become Successful and Wealthy.

OliverMaldonado.com

TheGreatestSalesBookInTheWorld.com

The

Greatest

Sales Book

in the

World

A Compilation of The Greatest Sales Presentations, Sales Scripts, Telemarketing Scripts, Rebuttals, Mailers, Referral Scripts and Tracking and Projection Reports The World Has Ever Seen!

This book could be worth $1,000,000.00 One Million Dollars to you!

By

Oliver P. Maldonado

WWW.OliverMaldonado.com
WWW.TheGreatestSalesbookintheWorld.com

About the Author

Oliver Maldonado has spent the past 12 years mastering the Art of Sales. He has traveled around the country consulting with companies and training salespeople. In his entire career he has been able to maintain a closing ratio above 90%. Oliver has trained regular people and converted them into great salespeople. His sales forces have all maintained a combined closing ratio of over 75%, right from the start.

www.ingramcontent.com/pod-product-compliance
Lightning Source LLC
Chambersburg PA
CBHW022131170526
45157CB00004B/1839